THE TEXAS LINK TO
Jerky Making

LARRY BURRIER

EAKIN PRESS  Austin, Texas

For CIP
information,
please access:
www.loc.gov

FIRST EDITION
Copyright © 2002
By Larry Burrier
Published in the United States of America
By Eakin Press
A Division of Sunbelt Media, Inc.
P.O. Drawer 90159 ☞ Austin, Texas 78709-0159
email: sales@eakinpress.com
💻 website: www.eakinpress.com 💻
ALL RIGHTS RESERVED.

1 2 3 4 5 6 7 8 9

1-57168-746-7

Contents

INTRODUCTION
All About Jerky

Ever wonder how jerky got to be called that? *Jerky* is actually a mispronunciation of the Peruvian Spanish word *charque* (pronounced "sharkey"), meaning dried or preserved meat.

As far back as 15,000 B.C., Arabia and Egypt made good use of the sun and warm winds to dry foods as a method of preserving. Indians of South and North America created similar techniques, and soon American settlers (if they hadn't already) learned to produce jerky.

The process was easy: Hunters would kill wild game for fresh meat and the remainder would then be thinly sliced and either hung in the sun to dry or stretched on sticks and smoke-dried over smoldering wood coals. This amazingly simple method of preserving provided ample supplies of meat for the early settlers to survive on as they journeyed cross-country. The dried meat would often be cooked with other foods not easily spoiled (such as potatoes, onions, beans) or boiled with rice or oats, or cooked separately in water, producing a meaty broth.

Jerky was and still is a lightweight and highly nutritious source of protein. And because it is a dried meat (at one-fourth its original size), it takes up far less space. As jerky has regained its popularity, the versatility of this product has also grown, becoming limited only by our imaginations! You can dry beef, venison, fowl, or fish and eat it just as it is or create a soup, stew, sandwich, or main course meal.

Drying or dehydration of meats is a method of preserving, by lowering the water or moisture content. The drying method keeps bacteria, yeast, and mold from forming and destroying the product. The benefits of dehydration include lower weight and smaller size, while at the same time creating a nutritious product with tremendous versatility.

Early pioneers probably didn't care about the fact that jerky made from lean meat is low in fat and cholesterol, or that this high protein meat is an excellent energy food. People today take jerky along for a quick snack while hunting, fishing, skiing, hiking, or biking.

Making jerky is fun and economical. And if you've ever priced bulk jerky products sold in retail stores or meat markets, you'll know that you stand to pay approximately $25 per pound for a good-quality jerky. But these products are too often over processed, oversalted, and in some cases even stale! Fresh jerky is much softer, holding far more flavor and nutrition.

Some important things to know about drying meats is that the process of "drying" requires low humidity and low temperatures of 90–150 degrees Fahrenheit; temperatures higher than this actually cook the meat from the outside, causing "case-hardening."

Low humidity, low temperature, and air current speed up the drying process for a better-finished product.

The difference between cooking and drying is the amount of time and the temperature to which the meat is exposed. Higher temperatures and shorter periods of drying time produce a hard, overdried piece of cooked meat, while low temperatures for a longer period of time will render a flexible, chewable piece of dried jerky.

The following pages will explain the different methods of drying jerky (using your household oven, barbecue smoker, home dehydrator, or microwave oven) as well as provide delicious marinades and recipes.

CHAPTER I
The Art of Making Jerky

Drying Methods

Oven Drying

After marinating your meat according to the instructions, remove your oven rack and place a small mesh wire on top. This will keep the meat from falling through. Preheat the oven to 140 degrees and place a cookie sheet or tinfoil below the meat rack to catch any drippings.

While the oven is preheating, space the meat strips on the wire mesh at least 1/4 inch apart to allow the warm air to circulate evenly. You can also use wood or metal skewers to hang the meat. Simply slide the skewers through the meat strips, then place each skewer on the oven rack so that the meat strips can hang between the rack openings.

After placing the meat in the oven, use a utensil or small wooden spoon to hold the door slightly open; this will allow the moisture to escape from the oven. After 1 hour, close the door completely for an additional hour, checking the meat every hour afterward. The jerky will be complete when there is little moisture inside the meat strips and they're flexible enough to bend without breaking.

The entire process should take approximately 3-4 hours, depending upon the thickness of the meat, humidity, and temperature.

Smoker Drying

Choosing to use the smoker method, as opposed to the oven-drying or dehydrating method, produces a far better, naturally smoked product.

After marinating your meat according to the instructions, preheat your smoker to 120-130 degrees by placing a small amount of water-soaked wood chips over the heat source. After the wood begins to cinder and smoke, place the wire meat rack at the opposite end of the smoker and away from the heat source.

Once again, you may want to consider placing a wire mesh on your smoker rack or using the skewer method.

Have the smoker damper completely open, and leave at this setting until the meat is dry to the touch, about 1 hour. Now, completely close the damper and readjust the heat to a lower temperature between 90-100 degrees. This will produce more smoke. Be sure to keep moist wood chips on the heat source, and *never* let the wood flame.

Smoke the meat for 2 hours, then remove the wood chips and continue allowing the heat to dry the meat. Most home-use smokers take about 6-8 hours to produce a good jerky.

Jerky is ready when little moisture is present and the meat is flexible enough to bend without breaking.

Dehydrator Drying

Household dehydrators are economical, lightweight, and require very little supervision. These are ideal for drying small amounts of jerky, approximately 2-3 pounds.

After marinating your meat according to the instructions, place meat strips on dryer racks, making sure that you leave a ¼-inch space between each piece.

Be sure that the dehydrator vents on the top cover are open, allowing moisture to escape for approximately four hours, after which time you should close the vent openings and continue drying until the meat has reached the desired dryness.

Most home dehydrators take approximately 12 hours (total time) to dry meat into jerky, but it's always best to check the meat every 4 hours, or until you're personally satisfied with the product.

As always, jerky is ready when little moisture is present and it is flexible without breaking.

Microwave Drying

Here's a quick way to make a small batch of jerky!

After marinating the meat according to the instructions, place the meat strips on a microwave roasting rack. Set the microwave on the highest setting for 4-6 minutes. After this time, you should notice moisture seeping out of the jerky; open the microwave and pat dry with a paper towel.

Continue to dry the meat in 30-second intervals until you notice a change in the meat's color (from brown to dark brown) and in its texture (from pliable to leathery). Jerky is ready when there is little moisture and it is flexible enough to bend without breaking.

Meats for Jerky

Jerky should always be made from lean cuts of meat, taking time to remove all fat, gristle, and membrane.

Some good choices from beef are:

Beef Skirts
Eye of Round
Sirloin Tip
Brisket
Inside Round
Flank Steaks.

There are many other meats that are excellent for making jerky:

Venison
Turkey
Chicken
Goose
Duck
Javelina
Rabbit.

Equipment for Jerky Making

· Large, clean cutting board
· 6"-10" sharp knife
· Standard set of measuring spoons
· Standard set of measuring cups
· Kitchen or bathroom scale
· Stainless steel, plastic, or glass casserole dish with lid for marinade
· 10"-long wood or metal skewers (for hanging meat slices)
· Large cookie sheet or pan (drip-pan)
· Nonstick spray

Do not use aluminum containers to mix or marinate.

Preparing Marinades

There are two types of marinade: *Dry Cure* and *Wet Cure.*

Dry Cure includes any variety of dry ingredients that please your particular taste; however, you will still need to add *curing salt* to any of your dry mixtures to guard against spoilage. The correct amount of curing salt is 1 level teaspoon per 5 pounds of meat.

With dry cures, you will use a layering process: laying meat slices in a dish and covering with cure, then placing another layer of meat and another covering of cure until the meat is covered completely. Cover the dish tightly with a lid and store in the refrigerator overnight. (Cures are formulated to penetrate meat at the rate of ¼ inch per 24 hours.)

Wet Cure is a solution of water, seasonings, and cure to marinate meats.

Mix all wet cure ingredients thoroughly in a large saucepan and bring to a light boil while constantly stirring. Reduce heat and allow cooling before pouring over meat.

Place meat slices in a large casserole dish, pour liquid marinade over meat, mixing thoroughly to assure a complete coating over all of the meat and a minimum of ¼ inch liquid covering the top of the meat. Place a lid on the container and refrigerate overnight. Again, cures are formulated to penetrate the meat at a rate of ¼ inch per 24 hours and may require a longer or shorter period of time, depending on the thickness of the meat slices.

Preparing Meats

After choosing which cut of meat you wish to use, collect all of your utensils and clean everything—your hands as well. Make sure that you have plenty of room to work, then lay your meat on a clean cutting board and trim off all fat, gristle, and membrane so that you have a pure, lean meat. This will produce a quality finished product.

Cut ¼- to ⅜-inch slices, the full-length of the meat, cutting with the meat grain. If you are unsure as to the direction of the grain, cut a test piece, taking each end in hand, and attempt to stretch the slice. If the meat separates into individual segments or pulls apart, you have cut across the meat grain. If the meat stretches, rather than pulls apart, you have cut with the meat grain.

Continue to slice into ¼- to ⅜-inch pieces until you have reached the desired number of pounds that you wish to make into jerky. You're now ready to choose a marinade recipe that best suits your taste.

Refer to page 9 for marinade directions.

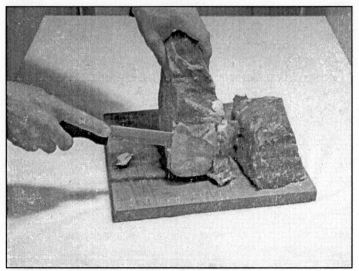

Place meat in freezer until slightly frozen. Remove cooled meat and trim all fat and gristle.

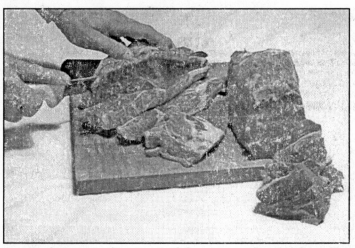

Locate the "grain direction" of the meat and proceed to slice with the grain in $^{1}/_{4}$– to $^{3}/_{8}$–inch-thick slices.

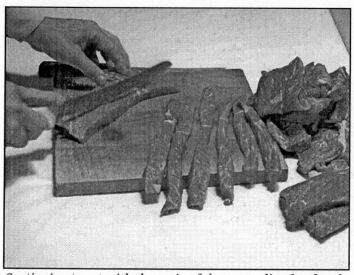

Continuing to cut with the grain of the meat, slice the already cut pieces into $^1/_4$ inch–$^3/_8$ inch thick slices.

Choose one of the marinade recipes provided and combine all ingredients in a large bowl, mixing well.

Place the meat strips in a large container with lid. Pour the marinade mixture over the meat, then seal the container and refrigerate overnight.

After the meat has marinated overnight, choose your dying method. If using the oven or smoker method, place the meat strips onto skewers on hooks. For the Oven Method, follow the directions on page 1, placing skewered or hooked meat (as seen in the photograph) on the oven rack of a preheated oven. For the Smoker Method, follow the directions on page 2, once again using the skewers on hooks to hang the meat.

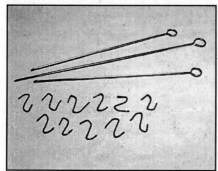

Meat skewers and meat hooks. Meat skewers are used to hang meat strips in oven or smoker. The small "S"-shaped hooks are easily made and used for hanging individual strips of meat in the oven or smoker.

Marinated meat strips hung on "S" hooks in the smoker.

Smoking Jerky

The temperature inside the smoker is very important and should be kept constant throughout the smoking or drying process.

There are two methods of smoking or drying: *Hot Smoking* and *Cold Smoking*.

Hot smoking temperatures should be maintained between 160–170 degrees and in most cases will produce "case-hardening." The finished product also has a shorter storage life.

Cold smoking is my preferred method. Cold smoking will produce a product that will keep much longer and will have less chance of producing "case-hardening." The temperature for cold smoking should be between 90–100 degrees. *A minimum or maximum amount of smoke has little to do with the quality of your jerky.* Ensure that the fire is always kept down to a smoldering bed of coals, never allowing the wood to flame.

Things to Know

- Jerky will develop mold: it is not completely moisture-free. If stored in plastic bags for a prolonged period of time, the meat will begin to mold. It is best to wrap and store any excess jerky meat in the freezer.

- Dampened wood chips make for a longer-lasting, pungent smoke, which gives the jerky a rich, smoked flavor.

- Never overfill your oven, smoker, home dehydrator, or microwave oven. This disallows proper air circulation, causing a longer drying period.

- Adding a fan to the drying process in a smokehouse will improve the drying time.

- Lean meat makes the best jerky. Meat considered lean is 99.9 percent fat free.

- Membrane, fat, and gristle that is not removed from the meat will produce a tough, chewy jerky.

- Curing salt (sodium nitrate) is used to prevent botulism, reduce spoilage, and retard bacteria growth during low temperature production. Usage amount is: 1 ounce per 25 pounds or 1 level teaspoon per 5 pounds of meat.

- Line "drip pans" with aluminum foil for easier cleanup.

- Meats dried for jerky shrink up to 50-60 percent during the drying process.
- An average 115-pound deer will yield nearly 25 pounds of prime, whole-muscle jerky meat.
- Fish jerky: It is best to use "firm" fish only to make smoked, dried jerky, such as red snapper, sea bass, swordfish, or shark.

CHAPTER 2
Jerky Recipes

The wet marinades included in this chapter are to be used in the jerky preparation directions as follows:

Directions

(1) Trim away from the meat as much fat, gristle, and membrane as possible.

(2) Freeze the trimmed meat for approximately 2-3 hours or until slightly frozen—this will make slicing easier.

(3) Slice meat into ¼- to ⅜-inch-thick slices.

(4) Choose one of the wet marinade recipes provided, mixing all ingredients thoroughly in a stainless steel, glass, or plastic casserole dish.

(5) Place meat strips in marinade mixture; cover and refrigerate overnight.

(6) Once the meat has marinated, spray your oven, smoker, or dehydrator racks with a nonstick spray and lay meat strips on the racks ¼ inch apart to provide for better heat and smoke circulation.

(7) Dry your jerky according to the instructions on pages 5-7.

Note: On all recipes, you may choose to lay out wax paper and sprinkle with coarse-ground black pepper, then roll the meat strips over the pepper before starting the drying process.

Country-Style Jerky

8 pounds Venison or Lean Beef
2 teaspoons Curing Salt
2 teaspoons Curry Powder
3 teaspoons Cayenne Pepper
4 teaspoons Black Pepper (table grind)
8 tablespoons Salt
3 tablespoons Onion Powder
2 tablespoons Garlic Powder
2 cups Soy Sauce
2 cups Worcestershire Sauce
3 cups Water

Pineapple-Style Jerky

8 pounds Venison or Lean Beef
2 tablespoons Curing Salt
8 tablespoons Salt
2 ½ tablespoons Ginger
2 teaspoons White Pepper
1 teaspoon Cayenne Pepper
1 cup Brown Sugar
5 cups Pineapple Juice
2 cups Soy Sauce

Orange-Style Jerky

8 pounds Venison or Lean Beef
2 teaspoons Curing Salt
8 tablespoons Salt
2 ½ tablespoons Ginger
2 teaspoons White Pepper
1 teaspoon Cayenne Pepper
1 cup Brown Sugar
5 cups Orange Juice
2 cups Soy Sauce

Louisiana Creole Jerky

8 pounds Venison or Lean Beef
6 tablespoons Garlic Powder
2 teaspoons Curing Salt
4 tablespoons Paprika
8 tablespoons Salt
4 teaspoons Cayenne Pepper
2 teaspoons Red Chili Pepper Powder
6 teaspoons Black Pepper
5 cups Water
2 cups Worcestershire Sauce

Louisiana Cajun Jerky

8 pounds Venison or Lean Beef
4 teaspoons Onion Powder
6 teaspoons Cayenne Pepper
6 tablespoons Garlic Powder
8 tablespoons Salt
2 teaspoons Curing Salt
2 teaspoons Red Chili Pepper Powder
2 teaspoons Oregano (whole)
6 teaspoons Black Pepper
2 teaspoons Ground Thyme
5 cups Water
2 cups Worcestershire Sauce

Chinese-Style Jerky

8 pounds Venison or Lean Beef
4 teaspoons Ground Coriander
3 teaspoons Ginger
8 tablespoons Salt
2 teaspoons Curing Salt
4 tablespoons Garlic Powder
4 teaspoons Black Pepper
2 cups Brown Sugar
3 cups Soy Sauce
3 cups cold Water
1 tablespoon Chinese Red Pepper Sauce
4 teaspoons Sesame Seed

Peppered Jerky

8 pounds Venison or Lean Beef

4 teaspoons Chili Powder

4 teaspoons Coriander

4 teaspoons Garlic Powder

8 tablespoons Salt

2 teaspoons Curing Salt

2 teaspoons Cayenne Pepper

6 cups Water

8 tablespoons Black Pepper (coarse-ground)—roll meat in
   pepper after marinating

Teriyaki Jerky

8 pounds Venison or Lean Beef

4 tablespoons Garlic Powder

2 tablespoons Yellow Mustard Seed (ground)

4 tablespoons Black Pepper

6 tablespoons Salt

2 teaspoons Curing Salt

1 cup Water

4 cups Teriyaki Sauce

1 cup Soy Sauce

Mesquite-Smoked Jerky

8 pounds Venison or Lean Beef

8 tablespoons Salt

10 teaspoons Mesquite Liquid Smoke

2 teaspoons Curing Salt

6 teaspoons Garlic Powder

4 teaspoons Black Pepper

3 teaspoons Chili Powder

4 teaspoons Cardamom

6 cups Water

Farmer's Jerky

8 pounds Venison or Lean Beef

2 tablespoons Onion Powder

2 teaspoons Curing Salt

8 tablespoons Salt

4 tablespoons Black Pepper (coarse-ground)

4 tablespoons Garlic Powder

4 teaspoons Paprika Powder

4 teaspoons Liquid Smoke

2 cups Worcestershire Sauce

1 cup Soy Sauce

2 cups Water

Italian Jerky

8 pounds Venison or Lean Beef

2 teaspoons Curing Salt

4 tablespoons Powdered Sugar

4 tablespoons Garlic Powder

8 tablespoons Salt

4 tablespoons Oregano Powder

4 tablespoons Dried Bell Pepper Flakes

4 tablespoons Thyme

2 cups Tomato Sauce

2 cups Worcestershire Sauce

1 cup Soy Sauce

1 cup Water

Texas Jerky

8 pounds Venison or Lean Beef

4 tablespoons Brown Sugar

8 tablespoons Salt

2 teaspoons Curing Salt

6 tablespoons Garlic Powder

4 tablespoons Onion Powder

2 cups Beer

1 cup Soy Sauce

1 cup Worcestershire Sauce

2 cups Water

3 tablespoons Tabasco Sauce

Hawaiian Jerky

8 pounds Venison or Lean Beef

2 teaspoons Curing Salt

3 tablespoons Ginger

8 tablespoons Salt

4 teaspoons Cayenne Pepper

2 tablespoons Cream of Tartar

¾ cup Brown Sugar

¼ cup Honey

2 cups Worcestershire Sauce

1 cup Soy Sauce

3 cups Water

Brown Sugar Jerky

8 pounds Venison or Lean Beef

5 teaspoons Liquid Smoke

3 tablespoons Ground Yellow Mustard Seed

8 tablespoons Salt

2 teaspoons Curing Salt

1 tablespoon Cayenne Pepper

2 tablespoons Black Pepper (coarse-ground)

2 cups Brown Sugar

2 tablespoons Garlic Powder

1 cup Honey

4 cups Water

Hickory Smoked Jerky

8 pounds Venison or Lean Beef

2 teaspoons Curing Salt

3 teaspoons White Pepper

3 teaspoons Black Pepper

10 teaspoons Hickory Liquid Smoke

8 tablespoons Salt

6 teaspoons Ground Yellow Mustard Seed

5 cups Water

3 teaspoons Cardamom

Hot and Spicy Jerky

8 pounds Venison or Lean Beef

6 teaspoons Cayenne Pepper

6 teaspoons Paprika

2 teaspoons Curing Salt

4 teaspoons Crushed Red Chili Peppers

8 tablespoons Salt

4 teaspoons Ground Yellow Mustard Seed

2 cups Worcestershire Sauce

5 cups Water

Curried Jerky

8 pounds Venison or Lean Beef

4 teaspoons White Pepper

6 tablespoons Curry Powder

5 tablespoons Salt

2 teaspoons Curing Salt

3 tablespoons Paprika

3 tablespoons Ground Yellow Mustard Seed

1 cup Honey

2 cups Soy Sauce

3 cups Water

Honey Jerky

8 pounds Venison or Lean Beef

6 tablespoons Salt

4 tablespoons Brown Sugar

2 teaspoons Curing Salt

4 teaspoons Coriander

4 teaspoons White Pepper

4 teaspoons Cinnamon

2 cups Honey

1 cup Soy Sauce

3 cups Water

Mesquite-Smoked Hot Jerky

8 pounds Venison or Lean Beef
5 tablespoons Salt
2 teaspoons Curing Salt
5 teaspoons Cayenne Pepper
10 teaspoons Mesquite Liquid Smoke
4 teaspoons Chili Powder
5 teaspoons Chinese Red Pepper Sauce
4 teaspoons Coriander (ground)
2 cups Worcestershire Sauce
1 cup Soy Sauce
3 cups Water

Jalapeño Jerky

8 pounds Venison or Lean Beef
6 tablespoons Salt
8 tablespoons Dried Jalapeño Flakes
2 teaspoons Curing Salt
4 teaspoons Garlic Powder
4 teaspoons Onion Powder
4 teaspoons Black Pepper
1 cup Brown Sugar
2 cups Worcestershire Sauce
4 cups Water

Old-Style Jerky

8 pounds Venison or Lean Beef

6 tablespoons Salt

4 tablespoons Garlic Powder

2 tablespoons Cayenne Pepper

2 teaspoons Curing Salt

10 teaspoons Liquid Smoke

4 teaspoons Coarse-Ground Black Pepper

8 teaspoons Sugar

4 cups Water

Jamaican Jerked Jerky

8 pounds Venison or Lean Beef

6 teaspoons Sugar

6 teaspoons Salt

2 teaspoons Curing Salt

3 teaspoons Ground Ginger

3 teaspoons Allspice

3 teaspoons Brown Mustard Seeds

3 teaspoons Ground Coriander

1 teaspoon Cinnamon

2 teaspoons Anise

6 teaspoons Lime Juice

5 cups Water

1 teaspoon Ground Habanero Chili

Bar-B-Q Jerky

8 pounds Venison or Lean Beef

2 teaspoons Curing Salt

4 cups Tomato Catsup

4 tablespoons Mustard

½ cup Brown Sugar

1 cup Worcestershire Sauce

4 tablespoons Coarse-Ground Black Pepper

3 tablespoons Garlic (minced)

3 teaspoons Vinegar

3 tablespoons Butter

4 tablespoons Minced Onion

4 tablespoons Salt

2 cups Water

Bourbon Jerky

8 pounds Venison or Lean Beef

2 teaspoons Curing Salt

4 tablespoons Garlic Powder

8 tablespoons Salt

4 tablespoons Coarse-Ground Black Pepper

3 cups Bourbon

2 cups Worcestershire Sauce

1 cup Water

5 teaspoons Paprika

Japanese Jerky

8 pounds Venison or Lean Beef

5 teaspoons Salt

4 tablespoons Japanese Pepper Sauce

2 teaspoons Curing Salt

6 tablespoons Honey

½ cup Sherry

4 tablespoons Sugar

½ cup Catsup

½ cup Oyster Sauce

½ cup Hoisin Sauce

1 cup Light Soy Sauce

1 cup Dark Soy Sauce

2 cups Water

Lemon-Pepper Jerky

8 pounds Venison or Lean Beef

8 tablespoons Salt

2 teaspoons Curing Salt

4 teaspoons Garlic Powder

6 teaspoons Black Pepper

3 cups Worcestershire Sauce

4 teaspoons Liquid Smoke

2 teaspoons Curry Powder

8 tablespoons Lemon Pepper

3 cups Water

Southwest Jerky

8 pounds Venison or Lean Beef
8 tablespoons Salt
2 teaspoons Curing Salt
4 tablespoons Black Pepper
2 teaspoons Cayenne Pepper
6 tablespoons Chili Powder
6 tablespoons Cumin
6 tablespoons Garlic Powder
6 tablespoons Dried Cilantro
4 cups Water
2 cups Worcestershire Sauce

Burgundy Jerky

8 pounds Venison or Lean Beef
8 tablespoons Salt
2 teaspoons Curing Salt
4 tablespoons Garlic Powder
1 cup Soy Sauce
½ cup Molasses
4 teaspoons Coarse-Ground Black Pepper
3 cups Burgundy
2 cups Water

Honey-Lemon Jerky

8 pounds Venison or Lean Beef
8 tablespoons Salt
4 tablespoons Garlic Powder
2 tablespoons Black Pepper
1 cup Honey
½ cup Lemon
2 cups Soy Sauce
2 cups Water
2 teaspoons Curing Salt

Camper's Jerky

8 pounds Venison or Lean Beef
8 tablespoons Salt
2 teaspoons Curing Salt
4 tablespoons Black Pepper
1 cup Brown Sugar
1 cup Worcestershire Sauce
1 cup Tamari Sauce
6 tablespoons Liquid Smoke
3 cups Water
1 tablespoon Cayenne Pepper

Javelina Jerky

8 pounds Javelina Meat

3 teaspoons Garlic Juice

8 tablespoons Salt

2 teaspoons Curing Salt

3 teaspoons Lemon Juice

1 cup Sugar

1 cup Soy Sauce

1 tablespoon Tabasco Sauce

4 tablespoons Black Pepper

4 cups Water

CHAPTER 3
Jerky Meals

Both you and your dinner guests will be surprised and impressed by the meals you've created using your own homemade jerky meats.

Jerky and Cheese-Rice

1½ pounds Dried Jerky
1½ cups Uncooked Rice
1 envelope Lipton Onion Soup Mix
1 10 ½ oz. can Cream of Mushroom Soup
1 ½ cups Water
2 cups Shredded Velveeta Cheese

Directions

Preheat oven to 450 degrees. Soak jerky in warm water for 10 minutes, then drain off water. Place uncooked rice in a greased casserole dish; add jerky and shredded cheese.

Sprinkle package of onion soup mix on rice and jerky, then add cream of mushroom soup.

Pour water over the ingredients; cover and bake for 45-60 minutes at 450 degrees.

Jerky and Pinto Beans

2 quarts Water
2 pounds Pinto Beans
¼ cup Diced Onions
1 can Rotel Tomatoes and Chiles
2 cloves Garlic—diced
½ pound diced Jerky
½ teaspoon Salt
½ teaspoon Black Pepper

Directions

Soak jerky in warm water for 10 minutes, then drain off water.

Soak pinto beans in warm water for 1 hour before cooking, then drain off water.

Bring the 2 quarts of water to a boil and add entire list of ingredients. Let boil for 30 minutes, then reduce heat and simmer for 1-2 hours, until the beans are soft.

Serve with cornbread.

Jerky Chili

2 pounds Diced Jerky

5 tablespoons Chili Powder

2 pounds Ground Beef

4 tablespoons Salt

2 tablespoons Paprika

½ cup Diced Onions

¼ cup Oil

1 can Tomato Sauce

1 quart Water

3 tablespoons Diced Garlic

1 teaspoon Cornstarch (for thickener)

2 tablespoons Black Pepper

Directions

Place oil in a skillet and add ground beef, onion, garlic, salt and pepper. Sauté ingredients until browned and transfer to a large pot, adding water, chili powder, paprika, and tomato sauce.

Simmer for 1-2 hours. Mix cornstarch with ¼ cup water and stir into mixture to thicken.

Serve with crackers or flour tortillas.

Jerky Stew

5 cups Water

2 cups Diced Tomatoes

2 pounds Diced Jerky

2 cups Diced Potatoes

2 tablespoons Diced Green Bell Pepper

½ cup Diced White Onions

½ cup Diced Carrots

2 cloves Garlic (shredded)

½ teaspoon Basil

1 teaspoon Oregano

¼ teaspoon Black Pepper

Salt to taste

1 teaspoon Cornstarch (for thickener)

Directions

Soak jerky in warm water for 10 minutes, then drain off water.

Combine water, jerky and all ingredients (except cornstarch) in a 2-quart pot. Cook over medium heat until it comes to a boil, then reduce heat and simmer for 30-45 minutes.

Mix ¼ cup water to cornstarch and add to thicken.

Jerky Stroganoff

1 ½ pounds Diced Jerky

½ cup Diced Onion

2 cloves Garlic (shredded)

2 tablespoons Butter

½ cup Mushrooms (sliced)

1 8-oz. can Tomato Paste

1 teaspoon Pepper

¼ teaspoon Salt

1 tablespoon Paprika

2 tablespoons Flour

1 cup Sour Cream

1 10-oz. package of Noodles

Directions

Soak jerky in warm water for 10 minutes, then drain off water.

Melt butter in a large skillet and add onion, garlic, salt and pepper. Sauté for 3 minutes, stirring occasionally. Add jerky and paprika, cooking for 2 minutes, then sprinkle in the flour, continuing to stir. Add tomato paste and mix well, simmering for 10 minutes.

Remove from heat and stir in mushrooms and sour cream. Heat thoroughly, but do not boil.

Cook noodles according to package instructions; drain and top with meat sauce.

Jerky and Cabbage Soup

1½ pounds Diced Jerky

½ cup Crushed Tomatoes

1 cup Diced Potatoes

½ cup Diced Onion

¼ cup Chopped Celery

½ head Cabbage

2 tablespoons Paprika

3 quarts Water

1 teaspoon Black Pepper

¼ teaspoon Salt

Directions

Using a medium-sized pot, bring to boil the water, jerky, tomatoes, onion, celery, and potatoes.

Reduce heat and add paprika, pepper, salt, and cabbage. Simmer for 1½–2 hours.

Serve with hard-crust French bread.

Creamed-Chipped Jerky

½ pound Shredded Jerky
2 cups Milk
¼ cup Diced Onion
½ teaspoon Minced Garlic
2 tablespoons Flour
Salt to taste
¼ teaspoon Black Pepper
½ cup Diced Carrots
4 tablespoons Oil
½ cup Water
½ cup Green Peas

Directions

Using a large skillet, heat oil and add onion, garlic, salt and pepper. Sauté for 2-3 minutes over low heat. Bring to a medium heat for 2-3 minutes, then add water and stir well. Reduce heat, continuing to stir, and add milk, shredded jerky, green peas, carrots, and flour. Continue to simmer until thick and creamy.

Serve over toast.

Fowl Soup

1 pound Shredded Turkey Jerky
1 can Chicken Broth
1 quart Water
¼ teaspoon Salt
¼ teaspoon Pepper
½ cup Barley
1 teaspoon Parsley Flakes

Directions

Using a 2-quart pot, add broth, water, salt, pepper, and barley and bring to a boil.

Reduce heat and add turkey jerky and parsley, continuing to simmer for 30-40 minutes, until barley is cooked soft.

Serve with hard-crust French bread.

Jerky Fajitas

2 pounds ¼-inch-thick Jerky Strips
½ cup Green Bell Pepper
1 minced Garlic Clove
¾ cup Diced Onion
½ cup Diced Tomatoes
3 tablespoons Oil
1 sliced Avocado
½ cup Shredded Cheddar Cheese
Flour Tortillas

Directions

Soak jerky in warm water for 10 minutes, then drain off water.

Using a large skillet, preheat oil over high heat. Reduce heat to medium and add bell pepper, garlic, onion, tomatoes, and jerky strips.

Sauté for 6–10 minutes, until cooked.

Serve on flour tortillas with sliced avocado, shredded cheese, and sour cream.

Optional: Hot Sauce.

Jerky Spud Boats

1 pound Shredded Jerky
4 medium Potatoes
½ cup Chopped Broccoli
½ cup Shredded Cheddar Cheese
½ cup Chopped Green Onion
1 cup Sour Cream
1 stick Butter (cut into teaspoon slices)

Directions

Preheat oven to 400 degrees.

Place potatoes in oven to bake until soft—about 45 minutes.

Remove baked potatoes and place on a plate, slicing in half.

Spoon broccoli, onion, cheese, butter, and sour cream onto the center of each potato and top with shredded jerky.

CHAPTER 4
Homemade Smoker/Dehydrator

An old refrigerator can be used to make a very efficient smoker/dehydrator and can smoke and dehydrate sausage and jerky meat very quickly.

The refrigerator used should be free of any plastic on the interior of the box, where the smoking and drying process takes place. Most old refrigerators have enamel/metal interiors.

Remove the compressor and motor and all box interior refrigerator parts.

Smoking/Dehydrating Instructions

Smoke sausage at 90 degrees for 4 hours, then turn off smoke generator and turn on the main heating element, adjusting it to 100 degrees. Adjust the air-circulating fan to the medium setting.

About 80-90 sausage links should dry in approximately 5-6 days, producing the same result as it would if the links were hung in a cooler or smokehouse for 21 days.

For jerky, smoke for 4 hours, using the same temperature and fan adjustments as used for sausage.

The 80-90 pounds of jerky meat should dry soft in about 10 hours.

Smoker/Dehydrator/Cooker

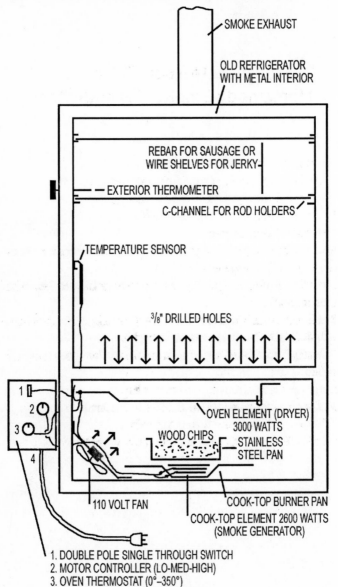

SMOKE EXHAUST

OLD REFRIGERATOR
WITH METAL INTERIOR

REBAR FOR SAUSAGE OR
WIRE SHELVES FOR JERKY

EXTERIOR THERMOMETER

C-CHANNEL FOR ROD HOLDERS

TEMPERATURE SENSOR

$^3/_8$" DRILLED HOLES

OVEN ELEMENT (DRYER)
3000 WATTS

WOOD CHIPS

STAINLESS
STEEL PAN

1

2

3

4

110 VOLT FAN

COOK-TOP BURNER PAN

COOK-TOP ELEMENT 2600 WATTS
(SMOKE GENERATOR)

1. DOUBLE POLE SINGLE THROUGH SWITCH
2. MOTOR CONTROLLER (LO-MED-HIGH)
3. OVEN THERMOSTAT (0°–350°)
4. 220 VOLT 30 AMP POWER SUPPLY

Materials Needed To Create
Homemade Smoker/Dehydrator

- Old Refrigerator
- 2-inch Pipe for Smoke Exhaust
- ½-inch C-Channel for Rod Holders
- ⅜-inch Rebar for Hanger Rods
- Exterior Thermometer
- Oven Thermostat with Temperature Sensor (settings 0–350 degrees)
- Double Pole Single Through Switch (for smoke generator)
- Bathroom Exhaust Fan Motor (for air circulation)
- 3000 Watt Oven Element (for dryer)
- 2600 Watt Cook-Top Element and Pan (for smoke generator)
- Stainless Steel Pan (for wood chips)
- 6x6-inch exterior Metal Box (for control mounting)
- #10 S.O. Cord for Power Supply
- 8 Pole Terminal Block (internal connections)